CITIES OF THE WORLD

ATHENS

BY R. CONRAD STEIN

CHILDREN'S PRESS®
A Division of Grolier Publishing
New York London Hong Kong Sydney
Danbury, Connecticut

CONSULTANTS

Fotios K. Litsas, Ph.D.
Director, Department of Education
Greek Orthodox Diocese of Chicago

Linda Cornwell
Learning Resource Consultant
Indiana Department of Education

Project Director: Downing Publishing Services
Design Director: Karen Kohn & Associates
Photo Researcher: Jan Izzo
Pronunciations: Courtesy of Tony Breed, M.A., Linguistics, University of Chicago

> NOTES ON GREEK PRONUNCIATION
> Most of the pronunciations in this book are exactly as they look, with the
> following notes: *th* is always *th* as in thing; *ts* is always *ts* as in gets; *ks* is
> always *x* as in tax, even at the beginning of a word; *gh*—the *g* sound in
> *gouri*—is a sound that does not occur in English. It's a relaxed *g* sound, sort
> of a gurgling noise. The closest sound in English is *g* as in go.

Library of Congress Cataloging-in-Publication Data

Stein, R. Conrad.
    Athens / by R. Conrad Stein.
     p. cm. — (Cities of the world)
    Includes index.
    Summary: Describes the history, culture, daily life, and points of
interest of Athens.
    ISBN 0-516-20300-2 (lib.bdg.)   0-516-26142-8 (pbk.)
    1. Athens (Greece)—Juvenile literature.   [1. Athens (Greece)]
I. Title. II. Series: Cities of the world (New York, N. Y.)
DF919.S83   1997   96-33277
949.5'2—dc20   CIP
                                                 AC

TABLE OF CONTENTS

The Acropolis of Athens is the most famous hill in the world. It was the crown of ancient Greek civilization. Look at the ancient buildings on the Acropolis and you behold beauty that has survived the ages. Rising above all the buildings is the Parthenon, which is almost 2,500 years old. Centuries ago, the Greeks led the world in theater, poetry, government, architecture, science, and art. At the height of Greece's glory, Athens was the most important of its cities.

Acropolis (UH-KRAH-PUH-LIHS)
Parthenon (PAHR-THUH-NAHN)

These women are among
the 4 million people who
make Athens their home.

It is wrong to think of Athens as a ghost
from the distant past, however. Walk to the rim
of the Acropolis. Gaze down and you see a
modern city where almost 4 million people live.
Men and women on the streets below rush to
and from their jobs. Children hurry to school.
Athenians live in two worlds. They are proud of
their city's history. But they know that Athens
is also the capital of the modern Greek
nation. Its residents focus their lives on
the promises and problems of the
world we all live in.

Athenian (UH-THEE-NEE-UHN)

Visitors to Athens can enjoy the riches of the past as well as the pleasures of today. Tourists seek out the monuments that made Athens the marvel of the world. Guests also delight in the food, the festivals, and the warmth of the Greek people. Most travelers to Athens begin their tour at the Acropolis. The hill holds more than ancient wonders. The Acropolis is a stunning landmark of a remarkable city.

The Immortal Acropolis

In the Greek language, the word *Acropolis* means "the town's edge" or "high place." The hill rises 512 feet above the rest of the city. Human beings have lived near the Acropolis for thousands of years. In primitive times, the steep hill might have been used as a defensive fortress.

In modern Athens, people go about their work as if in a race against the clock. Athenians try to separate their business life from their family life. Their business life is identical to that in any other industrial nation. Their family life is uniquely Greek.

THE CHILDREN OF ATHENS

Housing is extremely expensive for working people in Athens. Families of five or six often have to cram into a small apartment. The living room doubles as a bedroom at night. On crowded city blocks, children play jump rope on the rooftops. Athenian neighborhoods are close-knit. For that reason, youth gangs in Athens are never a problem. Street drug pushers do not exist.

Podosphero (soccer) is a passion among the boys of Athens. With little room to play, a parking lot serves as a soccer field. The red car at the end of the line is used as one goal. A green car at the other end is the opposite goal. Basketball is easily the second most popular sport among the city's youth. Greek national basketball teams always do well in the European championships and in the Olympic Games. Girls' basketball teams fill the stadiums during school competitions. Boys are the loudest rooters for their favorite girls' team.

At age six, an Athenian child begins a six-year grammar school program. Next, the boy or girl spends three years at the *Gymnasio*, a junior high school. Finally, the young person graduates to a three-year senior high school called the *Lykeio*. Nearly all students in the city—rich, poor, or middle-class—go to public schools. Private schools are few. Tuition and books are free in the public schools.

A Greek couple in an Athens park watch three small boys playing soccer.

podosphero (POH-DAHS-FEH-ROH)
Gymnasio (YEEM-NAH-SEE-OH)
Lykeio (LEE-KEE-OH)

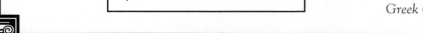

Greek workbook

The school system is a success story. Illiteracy is unknown among young people. The brightest students will go on to a university. The University of Athens is the nation's intellectual center.

Founded in 1837, the university trains future doctors, lawyers, educators, and engineers.

When she is six years old, the girl shown above will go to grammar school. When she reaches the age of the young woman shown at the right, she may attend the University of Athens.

Η σαλάτα.
ú-λι. Μαρούλι.
Ελιά.

CITY FAMILIES

Nothing is more important to a Greek than family. The house can burn down. Athens can erupt into bloody riots. But as long as family members remain in good health, a Greek thanks God for His blessings. Unquestioned love for children is the basis for family unity. Other elements, such as the roles of men and women, are changing in today's households.

An advertisement in a recent Athens newspaper announced, "Attractive woman, forty, with *proika* of a small flat near Plato Street, seeks husband." *Proika* is a Greek word meaning "dowry." It is a gift a man receives upon marrying a woman. The gift is presented by the woman's family. Years ago, a proika might have been a small farm or a fishing boat. Today, a small flat near

proika (PROY-KUH)

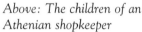

Above: The children of an Athenian shopkeeper

Left: A family celebration in the Plaka section of Athens

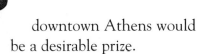

Right: A traditional Greek Orthodox wedding taking place at the Metropolis (Athens Cathedral)
Below: Two girls who attended the wedding share stories outside the church.

downtown Athens would be a desirable prize.

Many Greeks say the custom of proika giving is dying, especially in Athens. Feminists complain that paying a proika makes a marriage the same as a business transaction. Still, the practice lingers, and many families approve of it. The parents of a young bride happily give a proika in order to help the newlyweds buy furniture or perhaps make a down payment on a small house.

Only a generation ago, Athenian women were expected to stay home during the day. It was the woman's duty to keep the house spotless and the children on their best behavior. Children learned to fear the father and to run to the mother with their real or imagined hurts. In today's Athens, however, both parents often hold jobs. All family members have to pitch in with the tasks of cleaning and cooking.

Some Athenian fathers are saddened by their declining authority. A huge number of farm families have migrated to Athens in recent years. Many of the city's men grew up under

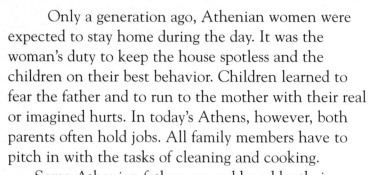

An Athenian cobbler at work

Men chatting at an Athens coffeehouse

Left: The hands of Athenian women are rarely idle. These family members are working on needlework projects during a pleasant afternoon.

Below: The owner of an Athens open-air market

farm society rules, where the father was the unquestioned family leader.

When feeling blue, Athenian men can escape to the neighborhood *kafeneion* (coffeehouse) for male companionship. In coffeehouses, men sip strong black coffee while they play cards or argue about sports or politics. Women rarely enter a kafeneion. It simply isn't done. The kafeneion is the last memory of the time when Athens and Greece were largely a man's world.

kafeneion (KAH-FEH-NEE-OHN)

FATE AND FAITH

Almost 2,000 years ago, Saint Paul visited Athens. He said, "Ye men of Athens, I perceive that in all things ye are too superstitious." Many observers believe Athenians are still plagued by superstitions. Lucky charms can be bought at the city's candy stores. Astrologers and fortunetellers do a booming business.

Other superstitions and odd customs abound. Consider the ritual you must go through if you accidentally spill the lemonade you are drinking with lunch. First, you must touch the spilled lemonade with your finger. Then you dab your finger behind your ear while saying, "*gouri*" ("good luck"). Another strange belief concerns scissors: Don't leave a pair of scissors open

gouri (GHOO-REE)

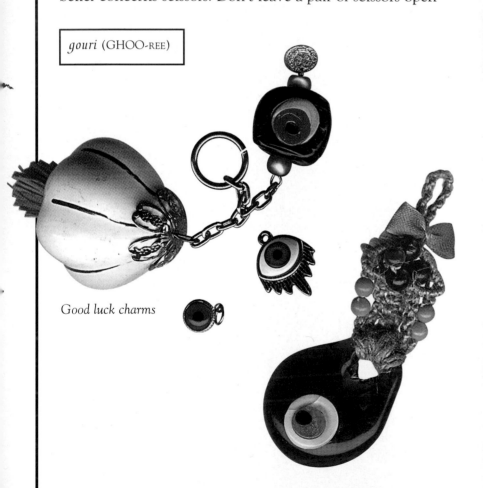

Good luck charms

Most Athenians belong to the Greek Orthodox Church. Crown Prince Pavlos (center rear) was married in a Greek Orthodox ceremony.

when putting them in a drawer. Why? Because open scissors lying in a drawer mean your neighbor will gossip about your family, that's why.

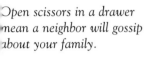

Open scissors in a drawer mean a neighbor will gossip about your family.

Educated Athenians laugh at the notion that their fellow citizens are overly superstitious. They say the people's flirtations with fortune-tellers amount to little more than harmless games. Besides, no fortune-telling wizard could

ever shake an Athenian from his true faith.

More than 90 percent of Athenians belong to the Greek Orthodox Church. The Easter season is the most sacred time of the year for the Greek Orthodox faithful. The season brings forth emotions that are at times joyful, and at other times almost painfully sad.

The Easter season is the most sacred time of year for followers of the Greek Orthodox faith. This priest is observing Good Friday in a city cemetery.

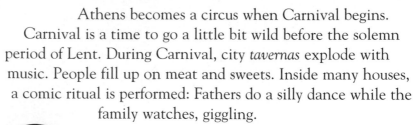

Assorted Greek olives

Athens becomes a circus when Carnival begins. Carnival is a time to go a little bit wild before the solemn period of Lent. During Carnival, city *tavernas* explode with music. People fill up on meat and sweets. Inside many houses, a comic ritual is performed: Fathers do a silly dance while the family watches, giggling.

Usually during February, the season of Lent begins. For the food-loving Athenian, this means giving up meat, sauces, and sweet desserts. Still, Lent starts with a pleasant holiday called Clean Monday. Family picnics are a Clean Monday tradition. Only sparse meals such as bread and vegetables or olives are eaten. At the

taverna (TUH-VARE-NUH)

A woman lights a candle inside a Greek Orthodox Church in Athens.

An Easter Sunday Game

Easter Sunday is a time for a family get-together and a huge meal. It is also a day to play a unique game. In Greek households, Easter eggs are hard-boiled and dyed red. A game is played by two children, each holding an egg. Gingerly, the children knock their eggs together. The one whose egg emerges without a crack wins the game. As a prize, the owner of the surviving egg gets to eat the opponent's egg.

Greek Easter eggs dyed red

picnics, boys and girls fly kites. So many kites soar over Athens on Clean Monday that their lines get tangled.

All of Athens is somber on the evening of Good Friday, when people mourn the death of Jesus Christ. On Holy Saturday, Athenians go to Midnight Mass. Near the end of the service, church lights all over the city dim. The stillness is frightening, like the end of the world. Then, at the stroke of midnight, the priest lights a candle. While bathed in candlelight, he cries out, "Christ is risen!" The people chant, "Indeed, He has risen!"

Parishioners march forward holding candles. They light their candles from a priest's candle, and then file out the door. Great candlelight parades weave through the streets. All over Athens, people herald the miracle: "Christ is risen!" "Indeed, He has risen!"

A Greek Orthodox priest

The monuments of the past are glorious ruins today. Looking at them stirs the soul with wonder. What was Athens like more than 2,000 years ago when it was the world's greatest city? Looking back to the distant past requires the gift of imagination.

A SPECIAL DAY IN OLD ATHENS

Imagine a very special day in the year 438 B.C. Today, the magnificent Parthenon will be officially open to the public. Athenians line the road that leads up to the Acropolis where the newly built Parthenon stands. A great parade begins. Young men riding horses lead the procession. Young women follow the men. The women chosen for this ceremony are the loveliest in the city. Musicians play flutes and harp-like stringed instruments called *lyres*.

Above: A fragment of the marble frieze (a sculptured band) that once went around all four sides of the Parthenon, which even now is the focal point of Athens and the Acropolis (below)

*The Parthenon
as it once looked*

Who watched this grand parade held so long ago? Nearly everyone in the entire city of 150,000 people would turn out for such a festive event. Knowing who was alive at the time, we can imagine who were the famous citizens witnessing the inauguration of the Parthenon.

Surely Phidias is there. Phidias is the city's greatest sculptor. He has designed and carved many of the statues and marble scenes that adorn the Parthenon. The scenes, called friezes, show heroic battles. Athenians battle against Amazons and gods fight giants. Greatest of the works of Phidias is the 38-foot-tall statue of Athena that stands in the center of the Parthenon. Athena's robe and shield are made of pure gold. The gold alone weighs more than a ton.

Phidias (FIGH-DEE-UHS)
Athena (UH-THEE-NUH)

A huge golden statue of Athena once stood in the center of the Parthenon.

A view of ancient Athens

The goal of the parade is the Parthenon building itself. The building possesses a majesty never seen before. Its roof, supported by gleaming white columns, seems to reach the sky. With mathematical precision, the Parthenon's 46 columns slant slightly inward to give the building a greater feeling of height. Engineers today estimate that if the columns were allowed to tower into the sky, they would meet about a mile above the base.

The philosopher Socrates no doubt watched the parade. In ancient Athens, philosophers were professionals, like storekeepers or doctors. Socrates is barefoot and his robe is shabby. Socrates once criticized

Ancient Athenians enjoyed horse races.

a student by saying, "You seem to think that happiness consists in luxury. . . . But I think to want nothing is to resemble the gods." Socrates teaches by endlessly questioning his students. His questions lead his listeners to see the illogic of their own arguments. Socrates is especially popular with the youth of Athens. Powerful leaders in Athenian society are jealous of Socrates' hold on the city's young people.

Marching at the head of the parade is Pericles. He is the city's political leader. It is not certain whether Pericles spoke during the inauguration of the Parthenon. Surely, one of his known speeches would have been appropriate for this golden moment: "Mighty indeed are [the city's] marks and monuments. . . . Future ages will wonder at us as the present age wonders at us now."

*Above: The market square
(agora) of ancient Athens
Left: A bust of Pericles*

Pericles (PARE-IH-CLEEZ)
Socrates (SAH-CRUH-TEEZ)

DAY-TO-DAY LIFE IN OLD ATHENS

Pericles led the city during a period called the "Golden Age of Athens." This period, which is also called the "Age of Pericles," extended from 461 to 431 B.C. It was a time when art flourished and when people learned not to live in terror of their gods. The Athenians practiced a revolutionary form of government called democracy. In their city, all male citizens had a voice in the decision-making process.

Philosophers in ancient Athens pressed each other with questions: "What is the universe made of?" "Why do people behave as they do?" Sometimes their answers touched upon realms never thought of before. A scientific philosopher named Anaxagoras argued that the sun is a gigantic burning rock, not a god as was widely believed.

Young men in Athens had the special mission of attaining excellence in athletics. On playing fields called gymnasiums, boys learned to wrestle, box, throw the javelin, and run as swiftly as the wind. Every four years,

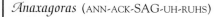

Anaxagoras (ANN-ACK-SAG-UH-RUHS)

Above: During the "Golden Age of Athens," people developed a new view of the gods.
Left: This vase was presented to the winner of a footrace at the Panathenaic Games held in honor of the goddess Athena.

26

the athletes of various Greek cities gathered to hold the Olympic Games. The games were almost a religious event. Even armies at war stopped fighting during Olympic festivities.

Athens society was not perfect at the time of its Golden Age. Women were not allowed to vote. One of every three Athenians was a slave. And city leaders turned on one of their prominent fellow citizens, the philosopher Socrates. Socrates prodded his students to question everything. When the students questioned government authority, however, Socrates was arrested on the grounds that he corrupted youth. After a trial, he was sentenced to die by poison. His famous student, Plato, gave a moving account of the great philosopher's death and teachings.

The death of Socrates is portrayed in this 1787 painting by French artist Jacques Louis David.

Plato (PLAY-TOH)

Souvenir bust of Socrates

CAPTIVE ATHENS

History teaches that golden ages are shortlived. These marvelous periods of achievement often end in war and disaster. Beginning in the 430s B.C., Athens waged a brutal series of wars against its Greek neighbors. The wars weakened all of Greek society and left the land open to conquest by foreigners. The Romans were the first of the foreign conquerors. Greece was later absorbed by the Byzantine Empire and later still occupied by the Ottoman Turks.

For more than 2,000 years, foreign powers held sway over Athens. Constant warfare reduced the once splendid city to a battered village. The ultimate blow came in 1687, when a Turkish warlord stored barrels of explosive powder in the Parthenon. A shell burst through the

After more than 2,000 years of war, the Greek War of Independence (1821-1829) finally freed Greece from foreign domination.
Left: A Eugène Delacroix painting, The Massacre of Chios, *1824*
Above: The Battle of Missolonghi, *1826*

roof, igniting the explosives. The blast tore off the Parthenon's roof and shattered its marvelous statuary. In one instant, the golden monument of the Golden Age was destroyed.

Greece fought a War of Independence from 1821 to 1829. The war finally freed the nation from foreign shackles. In 1834, Athens became the capital of the kingdom of Greece. By that time, only 6,000 people lived there. An English visitor remarked, "The least ruined objects [in Athens] are the ruins themselves." In 1941, the German army occupied the country. The Nazi swastika—the symbol of dictatorship—flew over Athens, the city where democracy was born. But Athenians knew that someday their city would rise again.

During World War II, from 1941 to 1944, the German army occupied Greece. Shown at left are German officers at the Acropolis.

The Captive Friezes

For more than 100 years, the remains of the Parthenon's statuary and friezes lay on the Acropolis grounds pretty much where they fell after the artillery blast of 1687. Then, in about 1800, British aristocrat Lord Elgin bribed an official of the Turkish government in Athens and was allowed to carry away the best of the ancient Greek sculptures. The magnificent marble carvings are now displayed at the British Museum in London, England. To this day, many Greeks consider it a disgrace that their national treasures stand in a foreign capital.

Think of the Acropolis as a stone. Throw the stone into a pond and watch the ripples made by the splash. Then imagine those ripples as Athenian neighborhoods. All the neighborhoods in the city radiate out from the Acropolis, the historic heart of Athens. Older districts lie near the hill. Newer neighborhoods are found in the distant ripples. South of the Acropolis, the ring-shaped pattern is broken where the city meets the sea. In other directions, the sprawling city of Athens ripples over the landscape.

Spilling down from the slope of the Acropolis is a fascinating neighborhood called the Plaka. It is a tangle of alleys and narrow streets. Tiny restaurants called tavernas line its sidewalks. The grounds of the Plaka have been inhabited for more than 5,000 years. But most Plaka buildings today date to the nineteenth century. This makes the buildings old by the strange double standard of Athens. While the city's monuments are ancient, the vast majority of its dwellings have been built in the last 200 years.

Near the Acropolis is the Agora, a collection of ruins as old as Athens itself. The word *agora* means "marketplace." In ancient times it was far more than a spot where people bought and sold goods. Athenians met

Plaka (PLAH-KUH)
Agora (AGG-UH-RUH)

Along the steep, narrow streets of the Plaka (right) are tavernas and market stalls like the one owned by this basket maker.

friends in the Agora. They debated philosophy and politics there. The Agora was a special place to worship the gods. Two major agoras lie in the neighborhood near the Acropolis. The second agora was built by the Romans, who conquered Greece some 2,000 years ago. Today, the Roman agora is sometimes called the "new" agora. After all, it is a mere 2,000 years old—new by the standards of Athens monuments.

Above: The Agora and the Temple of Hephaestus
Left: An Athenian woman shows off her hand-crocheted goods.

*Right: The Theater
of Dionysus
Below: The remains
of the frieze at the
Theater of Dionysus*

Dionysus
(DIE-UH-NIGH-SUSS)

On the southern slope of the Acropolis lies the Theater of Dionysus. The theater was built about 330 B.C. The ancient Greeks regarded theater as an art form. The Theater of Dionysus sat 15,000 people. Performances were attended by priests and poets as well as common Athenians. Now a highway roars with traffic just behind the theater's stage. The noisy highway serves as a reminder that Athens is a blending of the old and the new.

Uncovering Ancient Glory

The Theater of Dionysus, on the slope of the Acropolis, is a monument that was neglected for ages. After the decline of ancient Greek civilization, the theater was unused and eventually became covered over with dirt. Farmers grew fields of wheat over the once-magnificent theater. In 1838, excavations revealed the structure that had been loved by the Athenians of old.

THE MIDDLE RING

Old ways reach out to touch the new in Athens. The Agora was a meeting place in ancient times. Today, the city's squares serve as both marketplaces and community centers. The squares are created by a cross section of several roads. They are, therefore, a natural place for people to meet.

Two famous city squares are Omonoia and Syntagma. The squares lie in what can be considered the middle ripple of the city's neighborhoods. Many buildings in this middle ring were constructed hurriedly in the 1920s. The Greeks fought a disastrous war with Turkey from 1919 to 1923. Greece lost the war, and more than a million Greek nationals were forced to flee Turkish soil. Some 300,000 of those refugees settled in Athens. The city doubled in population in less than one year. The population surge of the 1920s was the beginning of rapid city growth that continues to this day.

Syntagma Square is also called Constitution Square. It features a circular fountain ringed by shade trees. At least a dozen sidewalk cafes serve customers in the Syntagma Square vicinity. Talk in the cafes turns to politics. Syntagma Square is a government center. The Greek Parliament Building rises nearby. Political demonstrations begin here. Many such demonstrations involve a million or more people. Sometimes the rallies turn ugly. Police and rioters have fought pitched battles in the normally peaceful Syntagma Square.

About twelve blocks away is Omonoia Square. This is workaday Athens. Omonoia Square has noisy markets and small shops. A jeweler in a

> Omonoia (OH-MUHN-OY-YUH)
> Syntagma (SIHN-TAG-MUH)

Colorful, busy Omonoia Square is filled with stores, fruit and vegetable stands, restaurants, and businesses.

Views of Syntagma Square

*Left: A sidewalk cafe
Below left: Communist students gather before a demonstration.
Below: A young boy feeding the ever-present pigeons*

store there might shout out that his rings are *"Kalo! Kalo!"* ("Good! Good!"). A baker might tear off a hunk of his bread and offer it to you as a sample. Most conversation in Omonoia restaurants focuses on business rather than politics.

Omonoia Square lacks the sophistication of Syntagma. But the open-air fruit and vegetable stands there are alive with the color of Athens.

kalo (KAH-LOH)

THE MODERN CITY

The outer ring—the largest of the three ripples—disappoints visitors. Modern Athens consists mostly of unimaginative buildings. Viewed from the canyonlike sidewalks, the buildings are little more than a collection of glass-and-concrete cubes.

The modern city exploded with people in the 1960s and 1970s. At the time, wages in Athens were about three times higher than a worker could earn in the farming villages. A flood of farm families moved to the city and created the outer ring. The outlying neighborhoods developed so fast that the city could not keep up with their needs. The number of motor vehicles grew from 200,000 in 1970 to almost a million by 1990. Yet no modern freeway system was built. Neither was the subway expanded. As a result, huge traffic jams in Athens are common. Also, the new neigh-

A view of Athens from the Acropolis

borhoods spread out with little space set aside for greenery. Only 3 percent of Athens is devoted to parkland. This means Athens has fewer parks than any other major city in Europe.

Every day, thousands of tourists land at Hellenikon Airport. The first neighborhoods they see are in the outer ring—a concrete jungle. Visitors should not judge the city too quickly, however. Beneath the hasty construction of recent years, Athens holds many hidden charms. First, it is a safe city. Athenians consider pickpocketing to be a major crime. They are appalled when they hear of the savage crimes that occur so regularly in the United States. Second, there are no slums and there are few homeless people. Greeks have strong family ties. They will readily take in an uncle or a cousin made homeless due to illness or job loss. Even in the drab outlying areas, people sweep the sidewalks and plant flowers in window boxes. Finally, Athenians are a warm and friendly people. They enjoy chatting with outsiders. Ask someone for street directions, and that person might very well invite you into the house for tea. In the Greek language, the word for "stranger"—xenos—is the same as the word for "guest."

xenos (KSEH-NOHSH)

A vendor selling snacks on an Athens street

very year, 7 million tourists visit Athens. Tourism is the city's prime industry. Most visitors want to see the city's famous monuments of the past. When not gazing with awe at ruins such as the Parthenon, they enjoy the many modern delights of the city.

THE PLAKA

There is no better place to take a walk than in the Plaka, the oldest neighborhood in Athens. It is one of the few parts of the city where cars are restricted. Pedestrians may stroll there without worrying about traffic. The Plaka consists of a thousand or so buildings. Most of the buildings have tiny stores at street level. The stores sell jewelry, candy, antiques, or souvenirs. Finding something to eat is never a problem. Two or three tavernas operate on every block. Greek food is so tasty it has skipped over oceans and crossed continents. Most Americans have sampled meals such as *dolmades* (spiced meat and rice wrapped in grape leaves). A Plaka restaurant is a good place to enjoy another Greek dish. Try crusty

Souvenir Grecian vase

Left: An Athenian street musucian
Below: A market stall in the old city of Athens

slices of *gyros* (pressed lamb and beef roasted on a huge skewer) with raw onions and *tzatziki*, a refreshing sauce of cucumbers in garlicky yogurt.

Athenians sometimes complain that the Plaka caters too much to tourists. Prices in many of its restaurants are steep. Music at the nightclubs is too often the pounding beat of American rock rather than the more mellow tones of Greek folk songs. But establishments frequented strictly by native Athenians are also found in the Plaka. There one hears the almost hypnotic music of the *bouzouki*, a guitarlike instrument. Greek traditional music is rarely performed without dance. Men and women dance. Men dance with other men. And men dance alone. When captured by the bouzouki beat, who needs a partner?

dolmades (DOHL-MAH-DEHS)
gyros (YEE-ROHSS)
tzatziki (TSAH-TSEE-kee)
bouzouki (BOO-ZOO-kee)

Above: Copper and brass items are sold at shops in the Plaka.

Left: Folk dancers at a Greek nightclub

Aristotle
(AIR-ISS-TAHT-UHLL)
Hephaestus
(HIH-FESS-TUHS)

The Temple of Hephaest

The ancient Agora lies in the Plaka. Walking in the Agora today thrills a visitor. Over this soil strolled Socrates, Plato, Aristotle, and the other giants of philosophy. Just outside the Agora stands the Temple of Hephaestus, built about 449 B.C. It is the best-preserved ancient temple in all of Greece.

Sea sponge

Sea sponge

The Tower
of the Winds

The Roman Agora is
also in the Plaka
district. An
enticing ruin
at the

Roman Agora is the Tower
of the Winds. Originally,
the structure was a combi-
nation sundial, water
clock, and weather vane.

Sea sponges from Greek waters are sold near
the Agora and other Athens tourist attractions.

PLACES OF INTEREST

Athens National Archaeological Museum is truly one of the world's great museums. It contains objects ranging from Stone Age tools to fine sculptures created by Greek masters. A highlight is the museum's Mycenaean Room. Mycenae was a city in ancient Greece. The city flourished 1,000 years before the Golden Age of Athens. In his poem *The Iliad*, the writer Homer claimed that the Mycenaean people fought a war against the city of Troy. During the war, the gods actually chose sides. The great god Zeus favored Troy. Zeus's wife, Hera, wanted the Mycenaean people to win. Because of this incredible interference from the gods, *The Iliad* was long regarded as a work of Homer's imagination. But in the 1800s, archaeologists found the ruins of Troy and precious items from Mycenae. Displayed in the Mycenaean Room is a brilliant gold death

Above: An artist sketching at the National Archaeological Museum
Left: An ancient sculpture on display at the museum

Rising above the tomb is the Greek Parliament Building. In the early 1800s, the building was a royal palace. The palace had a private garden, which is now a park called the National Garden. The park is a pleasant oasis in greenery-starved Athens. The garden has more than 500 species of trees and plants.

The Presidential Guard marching outside the Greek Parliament Building

The Greek Parliament Building was once a royal palace.

IN AND ABOUT TOWN

The city of Piraeus is about a twenty-minute train ride from downtown Athens. It is a port city, Athens's gateway to the sea. Docks in Piraeus are crammed with yachts owned by Europe's millionaires. It is also the place where tourists embark on cruises to the lovely Greek islands on the Aegean Sea. Piraeus is world famous for its seafood restaurants. Many of the restaurants have outdoor tables. A word of caution: the outdoor seafood restaurants are hangouts for an amazing number of stray cats. Feed these cats only at your own peril. A morsel of fish thrown to one cat means you will soon be swamped by dozens more.

Piraeus (PIGH-REE-UHS)
Aegean (IH-JEE-UHN)

The port of Piraeus is Athens's gateway to the sea.

Right: A fruit vendor at
Piraeus, the port of Athens
Below left: A Greek fisherman
Below right: Fishermen
mending nets at Piraeus

Lycabettus is a prominent mountain, which in ancient times stood well outside Athens. Today, city buildings surround the mountain. Athenians climb the 900-foot peak on paths that wind through groves of pine trees. At the top is a tiny chapel dedicated to Saint George. The peak also presents a sweeping view of the city. Often the view is not so pretty. On days when there is little wind, an observer from Mount Lycabettus sees a brown layer of smog covering the city. Athens, which is ringed on three sides by mountains, has the worst air-pollution problem of any city in Europe.

Lycabettus (LIH-KUH-BEH-TUSS)

Mount Lycabettus

Athenians are extremely polite with one another. If one man in a crowd accidentally steps on the toe of another man, both men will immediately apologize. But put an Athenian in a car and his civility disappears. Athenians are aggressive and rude drivers. Be especially careful when walking the streets of Athens. The polite driver is one who slows down before bursting past a stop sign.

Above: The Chapel of Saint George on the summit of Mount Lycabettus Right: A distant view of the Acropolis at night

Of course, the most famous mountain in Athens is the glorious Acropolis. Four major buildings, all constructed in the fifth century B.C., crown the hill. A visitor first encounters the Propylaea, which was designed to serve as a gate to this holy spot. To the right stands the Temple of Athena Nike, the Goddess of Victory. Some of the finest statues on this temple have been removed and placed in the Acropolis Museum, which is also on the hilltop. The statues were moved in recent years to protect them from air pollution. Beyond the temple stands the

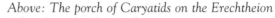
Above: The porch of Caryatids on the Erechtheion
Below (inset): The Parthenon
Below (54-55): A sweeping view of Athens at dusk

Erechtheion. Its most famous feature is the Caryatid Porch. The porch's roof is supported by six statues of lovely women. In the center of the hilltop rises the Parthenon. Gazing at this magnificent building, one can almost hear the words of Pericles: "Future ages will wonder at us as the present age wonders at us now."

The Acropolis is a proper place to end a tour of Athens. From its peak, one is amazed at the wonderful ancient structures. On its rim, one sees a huge modern city. This is Athens, a fantastic marriage of yesterday and today.

Propylaea (PRAH-PUH-LEE-UH)
Nike (NIGH-KEE)
Erechtheion (ih-RECK-thee-ahn)
Caryatid (KARE-ee-uh-tidd)

Paper model of the Temple of Athena Nike

FAMOUS LANDMARKS

The Temple of Athena Nike (on the right)

The Odeon of Herod Atticus

The National Archaeological Museum

Monuments on the Acropolis
Four ancient buildings built in the fifth century B.C. stand on the top of the Acropolis: the Erechtheion, the Propylaea, the Temple of Athena Nike, and the Parthenon.

Theater of Dionysus
Dating to the 300s B.C., the theater once seated 15,000 people for performances.

Odeon of Herod Atticus
Built about A.D. 160, this outdoor theater has been restored and is still used for special plays and concerts.

The Ancient Agora
The marketplace and meeting place of old Athens is now a large archaeological site, scattered with ruins.

The Roman Agora
Sometimes called the "new" Agora, this marketplace thrived when Rome occupied Athens roughly from the first century B.C. to the fourth century A.D.

Hadrian's Library
Another gift from Rome, the library was originally built in A.D. 132.

Temple of Olympian Zeus
The largest temple ever built in Greece, it was begun in 530 B.C., but not completed until Roman times, in A.D. 132.

National Archaeological Museum
The world-famous museum displays artwork from all periods of Greek history; the Mycenaean Room is particularly popular.

The Stoa of Attalus at the ancient Agora of Athens

The Temple of Olympian Zeus in the Roman section of Athens

The Greek Parliament Building

The Acropolis Museum
Standing on the Acropolis, the museum has nine rooms filled with statues and artworks taken from the Acropolis's complex of buildings.

Byzantine Museum
Houses religious items and treasures from the Byzantine Empire (A.D. 330-1453), which once embraced Athens and most of Greece.

National Garden
A refreshing island of greenery in the middle of the busy city.

Tomb of the Unknown Soldier
The unknown warrior resting in this tomb represents soldiers from all of Greece's recent wars; colorfully dressed soldiers called *evzones* guard the monument.

Monastiraki Square
Lying in the heart of an old market district, the square is home to street vendors and small shops.

Kolonaki Square
A fashionable residential neighborhood known for its cafes and elegant restaurants.

Monastery of Dafni
Standing about 6 miles west of downtown, this 1,500-year-old monastery is famous for its mosaic artworks from the Byzantine period.

FAST FACTS

POPULATION   1995

Metropolitan Area   3,670,000

AREA

City: 132 square miles

CLIMATE   Athens is rarely cold in the winter. The city has little snowfall, but the mountains that ring the metropolitan area are covered with enough snow that Athenians can ski there on weekends. Scant rainfall has hampered the city through the ages. Rain can be expected between October and February. The average July temperature is 79 degrees Fahrenheit; the average January temperature is 45 degrees Fahrenheit.

INDUSTRIES   Tourism is the city's number-one industry. The 7 million tourists who visit Athens each year provide jobs in hotels and restaurants. As the capital of Greece, Athens is also a prime source of government jobs. Factories in the city produce goods such as clothing, food products, electrical equipment, medicines, ships and ship parts, chemicals, and cement.

TRANSPORTATION   The nearby city of Piraeus is the major shipping port for Athens. Piraeus is one of the busiest ports in the eastern Mediterranean. Also busy is Hellenikon Airport, which serves Athens; some 11 million people a year pass through the airport. Athens has one major railroad line, which serves as the city's subway. Buses are plentiful, but frequently crowded. Traffic congestion is a chronic problem.

CHRONOLOGY

5000 B.C.
Neolithic people occupy the Acropolis; they may have used the flat-topped hill as a defensive fortress

1200 B.C.
The Trojan War; the rise of the Mycenaean Greeks

900 to 800 B.C.
Greek city-states, including Athens, rise to power

461 to 431 B.C.
Athens experiences its Golden Age

146 B.C.
Greece becomes a Roman province

A.D. 324
Athens and most of Greece become a part of the Byzantine Empire; Greek culture has a profound influence over Byzantine art and philosophy

A.D. 1456
Ottoman Turks capture Athens

1687
The Parthenon, being used to store explosives, is blown up by cannon fire

1821
The Greek War of Independence begins; the war eventually ends almost 400 years of Turkish domination over Greece

INDEX

Page numbers in boldface type indicate illustrations

TO FIND OUT MORE

BOOKS

Arnold, Frances. *Greece*. World in View series. Austin, Texas: Steck-Vaughn Library, 1992.

Dawson, Imogen. *Food and Feasts in Ancient Greece*. Parsippany, N.J.: New Discovery Books, 1995.

Dineen, Jacqueline. *The Greeks*. World of the Past series. New York: New Discovery Books, 1992.

DuBois, Jill. *Greece*. Cultures of the World series. New York: Marshall Cavendish, 1993.

MacDonald, Fiona and Mark Bergin. *A Greek Temple*. Inside Story series. New York: Peter Bedrick Books, 1992.

Moessinger, Pierre. *Socrates*. Mankato: Creative Education, 1992.

Nardo, Don. *The Age of Pericles*. World History series. San Diego, Calif.: Lucent Books, 1995.

Raphael, Elaine and Don Bolognese. *Drawing History: Ancient Greece*. New York: Franklin Watts, 1989.

Villios, Lynn W. *Cooking the Greek Way*. Minneapolis: Lerner Publications, 1984.

Waterlow, Julia. *Greece*. Our Country series. New York: The Bookwright Press, 1992.

ONLINE SITES

Ancient City of Athens
http://www.indiana.edu/~kglowack/Athens/Athens.html
Many images and much information about the history of Athens and Greece, as well as "visits" to the Agora, the Acropolis, and other sections of Athens

Ancient Greek World Tour
http://www.museum.upenn.edu/Greek_World/Intro.html
Go back in time to discover artworks and artifacts as you learn about the land and time, daily life, the economy, and religion

Ancient Olympic Games Virtual Museum
http://devlab.dartmouth.edu/olympic/
Take a virtual tour of the museum, learn about the ancient contests, hear stories, and see a slide show on modern Greece

ArtServe
http://rubens.anu.edu.au/
View more than 16,000 images of art and architecture from the Mediterranean Basin, including works from Greece, Italy, France, and other nations

Athens
http://one-world.net/hellas/attica/athens.htm
Take a tour of Athens, visit archaeological sites, learn some history, and find out how the city got its name

Athens News Agency
http://www.forthnet.gr/ape/
Get today's news—or research recent news—in Greek or English

Athens: The Akropolis
http://www.vacation.forthnet.gr/
A tourist guide to Greece that includes visitor information as well as the history and architecture of the many famous ruins of the Acropolis

Greek Mythology
http://www.intergate.net/uhtml/.jhunt/greek_myth/greek_myth.html
A "who's who" of Greek mythology, with many stories and pictures

Perseus Project
http://medusa.perseus.tufts.edu/
An interactive multimedia site focusing on ancient Greece. Learn about various sites, artifacts, the ancient Olympic Games, and much more

ABOUT THE AUTHOR

R. Conrad Stein was born in Chicago. After serving in the Marine Corps, he attended the University of Illinois, where he received a degree in history. He later studied in Mexico. The author has published more than eighty history books for young readers. He lives in Chicago with his wife and their daughter Janna. Traveling the world is Mr. Stein's passion. He has been to Athens, and considers it one of the most interesting cities he has ever seen.